SAINT TORCH

New & Selected Poems

SAINT TORCH

New & Selected Poems

Emily Fragos

Sheep Meadow Press
Rhinebeck, New York

Designed and typeset by The Sheep Meadow Press

Distributed by The University Press of New England

Author Photograph: Yuka Urushibata
Cover art: Judith Scott, detail, Untitled (1988/89). Permanent
    Collection, Creative Growth Art Center.
Cover photograph: Leon Borensztein

Library of Congress Cataloging-in-Publication Data

Names: Fragos, Emily, author.
Title: Saint torch : new & selected poems / Emily Fragos.
Description: Rhinebeck, NY : Sheep Meadow Press, [2017]
Identifiers: LCCN 2017019039 | ISBN 9781937679767 (pbk. : alk. paper)
Classification: LCC PS3606.R345 A6 2017 | DDC 811/.6--dc23
LC record available at https://lccn.loc.gov/2017019039

All inquiries and permission requests should be addressed to the publisher:

The Sheep Meadow Press
PO Box 84
Rhinebeck, NY 12572

For my sisters, Helen and Elizabeth

CONTENTS

SELECTED POEMS FROM *HOSTAGE*

ACKNOWLEDGMENTS

The author wishes to thank the editors of the following publications where these poems originally appeared, sometimes in slightly different versions.

The Boston Review: "Medium"/"The Fortune Teller"

The Denver Quarterly: "Haze," "Robert Walser," and "Terminus"

Five Points, Journal of Literature & Art: "Goya's Mirth" and "The Laundry Room"

The Harvard Review: "Théâtre de l'Odéon"

MiPOesias: "The Letters of Emma Hauck"

The New Republic: "Ponies at the South Pole"

Ploughshares: "After Dürer"

Poem-A-Day/Academy of American Poets: "The Sadness of Clothes"

The Threepenny Review: "On Robert Walser"

The Yale Review: "Inventory of the Royal War Paintings"

"The Sadness of Clothes" appeared in *Best American Poetry 2016*, guest editor, Edward Hirsch

"After Dürer" appeared in *Poems of Gratitude*, The Everyman's Pocket Library

"Boardwalk in Winter" appeared in the anthology, *The Traveler's Vade Mecum*

A special thank you to Stanley Moss, my publisher and fellow poet, for his loving and caring support of me and my work.

SAINT TORCH

Man, when he does not grieve, hardly exists.
—Antonio Porchia
tr. W.S. Merwin

THE SADNESS OF CLOTHES

When someone dies, the clothes are so sad. They have outlived
their usefulness and cannot get warm and full.
You talk to the clothes and explain that he is not coming back

as when he showed up immaculately dressed in slacks and plaid jacket
and had that beautiful smile on and you'd talk.
You'd go to get something and come back and he'd be gone.

You explain death to the clothes like that dream.
You tell them how much you miss the spouse
and how much you miss the pet with its little winter sweater.

You tell the worn raincoat that if you talk about it,
you will finally let grief out. The ancients forged the words
for battle and victory onto their shields and then they went out

and fought to the last breath. Words have that kind of power
you remind the clothes that remain in the drawer, arms stubbornly
folded across the chest, or slung across the backs of chairs,

or hanging inside the dark closet. Do with us what you will,
they faintly sigh, as you close the door on them.
He is gone and no one can tell us where.

PONIES AT THE SOUTH POLE
after a photograph, Scott Expedition, 1912

They are quieter than quiet. They are colder than cold
can be imagined. They may very well be blind.

Their ears receive the last sensation, a tiny crumble
of nothing. Their oblong heads tilt toward each other.

       . . . the end cannot be far writes the bungling,
stubborn man in his battered white tent,

writes suffering, bungling man.

MY BODY

The body she needs me now to cut her food and feed her,
to bring the glass of sweet water, never sweeter, to her mouth,
dry and shuttered. Now it unfurls itself as mouth, fish wet
and bird ascendant to a higher branch, with the taste of peaches
on its tongue, and for a moment she is mine again. The body
she needs me to hold her hand in the antiseptic rooms, the pill-clicking
halls, the ill surrounding her with their ugly eyes surrounding her.
Needs me to massage her neck, her legs, her temples so filled with
ancient *agonia*. Her breathing is shallow now, more so than yesterday.
I alone can tell. She needs me to call her back. She grows evermore
distant, ever deeper, too tired to lift her head, her arms, to speak
the barest of words. I alone know what is happening. The body
she requires me now full force to her kind attention.

AFTER DÜRER

As when icy illness ends that you never expected
    Could possibly end, and the terrified body, enveloped
In warm water, reposes, you could kiss every child on the hand,
    Every leaf in the forest, every stone of the wall. A low moan escapes
The mouth. Melancholia, the accompanying spirit, is departing with
    Her ratty wings and crusted eyes, her suitcase of rocks.
A shy, small creature steps trembling from the brush.

AT THE BURNING OF SAINT TORCH

In my father's fields, tired hands spread manure,
owlets scream in their nests, scaring the children

with the sounds of their wild lives, and the great,
patient oxen pull, pull . . .

A path is being cut through the throng for my cart
and the dancing bear with a ring through its soft nose.

His beautiful fur is wet and glistening.
I enter the delirium like a child enters the playroom,

deaf to the surface of things.
With your last body, pray for the beasts,

to be yoked together with them, to stumble
with them, to be halted, to be rested.

TO WALT WHITMAN ON HIS MAY 31ST BIRTHDAY

So many dogs went by with their people and they were happy to be walked,
sniffing at scents, accustomed to the route.
One stopped right in front of me and crouched on skinny legs, a tiny silver-gray

poodle with a patient human, and I watched a brown cigar of poop
come out of its behind. Then it stood up and gave a little Janis Joplin backward
    kick
and waited for the silent young woman to clean up after it and away they went.

I almost applauded for them, almost shouted Encore!
Mexican delivery boys sped by. A shuffling man in huge black shoes went by.
No one noticed him or the dark woman who cared for him.

I felt like Walt Whitman while I sat on that bench and watched life run its
    course.
Is it true that he piled his belongings in the center of his Camden room and used
    a fishing
pole to hook things and bring them to him, in pain, incontinent, near blind.

Wonderful to depart;/Wonderful to be here! I celebrate you,
dancing poodle, old man and tired aide, solemn delivery boy on your clunky
    bike—
chicken with broccoli, noodles and egg roll—swift on your way.

GOYA'S MIRTH

1.

Can you hear them shrieking, the filthy witch and the crackly-
skinned insect, slurping bread soup and rising from the table of crusted
    ladles
to dance, damn it, leaping in midair, kicking grief in the fat gut.

2.

Who stinks here?
It is I, Lord, reeling under these heavy, misshapen clothes.
The world waves a fan in front of its nose.
It is the cancer, it is the dying off. It is I, your foul, offensive lady,
your mossy rock. I have a need to stop it, but I cannot.

3.

Push your cart up and down the street. No one sees you, mémère, but you are
    safe here
in Francisco's wild drawing. Forget the words, forget the worms. A dog scrap
    rolls under
the table, forgotten. The dog? You will lie with him soon.

GOYA GAZED

Lunatics rave.
A portly man lowering
Himself onto a toilet-hole
Presents the mooniest
Buttocks ever. A young
Bruja hoists herself
Aloft with a rope
Looped under her feet,
Her nails grown wild.
Wings have been strapped
To a little dog in the sky.
They snap and he
Plummets earthward.

May I never find myself
Lost in his abyss of deafness
And horror. May I never, dear god,
Live beyond sadness.

THE LAUNDRY ROOM

Something about the woman
Who never speaks. The slow movements
As if in a trance, the awareness of me

Behind her, moving forward with my basket of clothes.
This is no longer the dull, pleasant
Laundry room in the newly painted gray

Basement. This is unchangeable time.
Holding the underwear and blackened
Socks, she has relinquished the one

Her heart has been waiting for.
You can see that she held out for a long spell,
Letting a smile pass through her narrow lips

At the supermarket, at the pharmacy,
Where she picked up her headache pills, her
Special soaps for sensitive skin,

Dreaming of warm people,
Some naked, some in flowing caftans,
Walking about on beautiful legs.

THE LETTERS OF EMMA HAUCK*

Come the labyrinth,
come the curdling word, the black ladder,
that tears a hole through the asylum's roof,

troposphere, stratosphere, to make for us
our own anesthesia, lullaby-and-goodnight,
sweet love. Pleased to wear rags around the mouth

and nose to contain the last essence from seeping,
weighted down by gauze, just barely, to keep
us here, by what kind of what.

*Emma Hauck was committed in 1909 Germany for schizophrenia. She
wrote many letters to her husband, saying only, "Sweetheart, come,"
thousands of times. None were ever delivered. Her letters are now
famous examples of "outsider" art.

LEGEND

They will come in a little boat when it is all over
and we are disappeared from this earth, this blessed lighthouse,
to find our winter coats on their pegs and dinner plates washed
and neatly stacked, beds made, one chair at the table tumbled over
in haste, they will surmise, as *man overboard* caused one of us to rush
outside and be swallowed up with the others. The crate of thick rope
unraveled down below so, yes, they will say, it was the tide, a freak wave,
brutal and sudden and stunning as all misfortune, that swept our bodies away,
never to surface, for a hundred years. They swear they can hear us moan
out in the dark, unfathomable waters, as they hurry to where they are going.
They say we are become creatures, with our faces blanked out,
our mouths opening and closing like fish, our skin replaced by brine;
but we are lightsmen, masters of tides, of ropes, of winter coats
and lighthouse loneliness and here is what happened to us:
death came with the sound of ten thousand horses galloping,
breaking down the wall, and chatterbox, confessional Ducat
went quiet and McCarthy and I were crying.

SNOW DIARY/1846

Father saw thin tracks and followed them but found only wild, fleet deer
leaping majestically out of the mounds . . .

Brother heaves the axe more than anything else with such beauty . . .

Huge birds with wings ten feet across soared above our heads and melted
      into the milk-white
sky. Would I were a bird with wings to get about! . . .

The mules fall head first into the drifts and are too tired to get up. Our
      fathers yoke themselves
to each other and lash themselves to the heaped pallets which they pull
      like bullocks . . .

All our eyes are turning blue . . .

We are close, we are close, I say to my friends, who, dark and dumb, can
      no longer . . .

I tumble into California and place my feet slowly, methodically, in the
      right way
so that I might seem a bright young thing again . . .

I am to marry a good man and live in the golden, sumptuous sun that sings
      a mid-stream, that
sings a full tilt without my once done asking . . .

O, my lost ones, days no one knows when the weakness comes over me . . .

IKTSUARPOK*

to rise
from the bed
to go into
the cold
to wait for
the one
who does
not come

to hear
the snow
squeal
beneath
your feet
to see
your breath
fume
to feel
your heart
beat
to look
left
then right
for the one
who is
coming
who does
not come

to sit at
the table
to stare
at the door
for the
one
who is

coming
who does
not come

to go far
far
into
the dark rock
to go deep
deep
into
the cold sea
to look for
the one
who does
not come

*The poem is an interpretation of this single Inuit word.

REUNION

There was the guy from Ronkonkoma who lived for souvlaki.
There was the precocious Smithie who worshipped Dostoyevski
and sobbed when the Republicans won.

There was the blabber mouth with a million cats
and the tender-hearted boy with rotten teeth and the nurse's
cheating husband . . .

Are they well? Are they oddly where I left them?

And while we're here, what happened to the girl sleeping face down
on the sidewalk, arms and legs splayed, or once, jubilantly
pointing at kaiser rolls and liverwurst at the deli,

waving a dollar bill around in her filthy hand.
Man, what a stench! If I ever get that bad, a tubby guy
said too loudly as he held his nose,

effen shoot me, bro. What became of that guy
and his sullen bro and the sports nut working the slicer
with Band-Aids on his fingers. Does anyone know?

Do they all still have their fingers and toes,
their one chance at being alive,
on the cusp of a soft-petal fall from this earth?

THE FORTUNE TELLER

Rest

In back alleys and side streets and along the tracks at night alone
or with one other, trudging. On their backs, black garbage bags

stuffed with filthy towels, a mechanical canary, a small wooden
model of a Bavarian castle, biscuit tins, the harp of a lamp . . .

The lumberyard psychic pulls out her sofa bed that kills her back
and puts away her tea cup and manuscript of astral charts.

At the end of this night, you will find the place to lie down
and be still at last, hosts coming alive like trees in a fairy tale

to help unpack your belongings and there will be warm food,
a baby asleep in a deep, soft ball, and there will be scratchy music.

Grace

The childlike sun is melting you, strong on your arms,
rose mouth, and cheeks. The stones of the vertebrae

are growing smooth and you want nothing more added
to your pockets, bookshelves, damp cellar with its one

scary light bulb. How grateful you are for your warm bed.
All who are seated are pulling away in neat, silent rows.

A great wave is carrying them into a far distant corner,
but wait, look, they are floating out the window, saved,

one by one. Under the swarm, the black ribbon of sky,
you hear the night thief in his grinning cat mask

slip through the line of trees and break into the dark
houses, just to hear the sleepers breathing.

Dying

Something warm is being placed in your hand, a fragment
of indecipherable writing, the mystical power of letters

being liberated from their barns.
That is the Great Pyrenees you've always loved, bounding away

before you can command your frozen hand to rise.
Those are twirling, laughing children you hear.

She leans her head against yours, bare tree
to bare tree, and is consoled.

Sleep floating, love, and when limbs touch nothing,
you will lose the earth.

Hundreds of thousands of horses
are running toward you. They are breaking down the door.

ON ROBERT WALSER

You saw a dwarf and imagined yourself dwarf
or the old, homeless hag, pushing her cart of junk.

You closed your eyes for days at a time,
groping along the village walls, tumbling into bushes
with an embarrassed gasp.

You adored the gentlewoman in her riding habit
and the chattering birds with faces like walnuts
and feet like twigs, so alive, alert, and active

in their birdie pursuits. Standing alone in your stale,
furnished room, you felt a shudder of feather
and the glowing air grew full, so close. To be alive

was wonderful, but *to be small and to stay small --*
drop of water into the water.

ROBERT WALSER

From barracks of pandemonium, from footpaths of solitude,
Be glad, be gentle and kind/Patient

And the asylum aide, carrying a lantern,
Stumbling upon him in the meadow's lit snow,

His hat flown from his head, his eyes locked open
In doll-like wonder. How unexpected is death, how expected.

HAZE

The seeing-eye dog folds himself behind the master's
long, thick legs. He is stuffed back there. His eyes,
pitying and sorrowful, are indentured servants

to the master's grand illusion . . . the master, whose feet
stink like cabbage in big black shoes and whose eyes
float without roots or peace, ghost ships in a milky ocean.

SO QUICK BRIGHT THINGS COME TO CONFUSION

The clip clop of the horses' hooves as the carriage pulls up.
The weary visitor in his grey waistcoat steps out. He is here
For a visit to an old school chum, a Count in a castle, no less.

He is expecting an admired life, a career in the law, rising to
Chief Magistrate, a handsome son to hunt with in the country.
They will wear matching wellies, green, with lamb's wool

Interior. How fine and contented those strolls shall be, a loyal
Shepherd dog at their side. It won't take long -- one evening
At the dinner table piled with venison and blood-red goblets,

A large loaf of stale bread he will find surprising, but only after.
He will be lucky to get out of there with his life, any kind of life,
An orphan, a chimney sweep, a one-legged beggar in London

He'd be grateful for. Mercy, turn around, man, but man
Just strides through that massive door that is bolted behind him
And holds out his hand as nearness and affection require.

INVENTORY OF THE ROYAL WAR PAINTINGS

The warm piss in a dead ear.
The hamstring stretch of a leg

twisted under her, the strung hands
going numb. The fleeing girl's

seared flesh, the shamed faces
turned away from us with grief

in their necks' pulsing cords.
Muzzle the scurvy dogs! the soldier

shrieks, up to his knees in muck.
From the glacial, muttering fields,

here comes cretinous Death
in his grinning black-cat mask,

riding a flying, red-plumed horse.
Catapults arch like vultures.

IKON

Her downcast face is etched in the bread

By the toaster's black char. Her son, pulled down

From his agony on Earth, lives in the shower mold,

On a dog's rump, banana peel, rotting tree stump.

Locked inside these strange bodies, they bring comfort

To the frightened, the going-blind, who line up to touch

Their enormous, broken eyes; their exhausted, empty mouths.

Behold, Mary, your child rides piggy-back, washing ashore

On the skin of a dead squid, crossing the dew-slicked

Meadow on the carapace of a little turtle.

THÉÂTRE DE L'ODÉON

I could not rise from the dark and go out into the cool,
night air of that beautiful city,

could not get on with my conniving, young life.
What had been smooth and good became impossible, slowly,

meticulously, placing one foot in front of the next,
so that legs, as if buried in snow, might inch along the river

and the alleys with the clochards and the cats,
and I might seem a bright young thing again.

All this before the shock of loss, the dying, who linger
with their weak bodies and blank faces,

and my own stupid share of human harm
inflicted upon the innocent,

and long before Time, that asp,
started laughing, *laughing* at me.

PLEASE INFORM THE MAYOR

Among other summer things, I dread backyards.
They are out there until all hours, howling
their heads off like hyenas,
barbequing steak at midnight.
You can hear people yelling at them from open windows,
shut the hell up, but they keep right on going
with their partying and their loud music
and their applauding for the young niece
doing ballet in her red leotard. (Little do they know
how uncentered is her line, how sloppy
are her long limbs. Little do they know.)
All I ask for is a little peace,
high above them in my room, to enjoy
a book, my shows, or to do a crossword puzzle
by the lamp. What is the capital of Tibet? What is
Thomas Edison's middle name? What is another word
for pickleball? Who can help me.
I am closer to the end than I am to life.
You know what I mean.

GRAND OPENING

Into a vacant space, the restaurant takes shape.
Small round tables, chairs, white table cloths, paintings
of rustic villages, a fresh green awning and they are ready.
Night after night the blonde wife and children of the Russian
sit at the tables with plates of food in front of them, staring
through the window at people who do not care to enter.
Their plates become like begging bowls extended.
Then even they stop coming and the tables stay empty.
The dogs don't like the dog food, the husband screams.
He had not known he could be so defeated,
as if by the grandmaster of chess he had seen as a child
who had found the perfect combination to crush
his opponent's mind. He remembers how he had walked
like a zombie in imitation of the loser's stunned exit
from the stage. *Me now*, he breathes, the used-up
man, sitting on the curb with his head in his hands.

TERMINUS

We take buses everywhere together, careful to retrieve
what is left behind. Our stale room fills with abundance:

hats of all sizes, a fine silk scarf, books with curious marginalia,
black umbrellas, eyeglasses for the near- and farsighted,

and even a gray parrot tethered to a stick. *Hello, darling,
how was your day*, he calls out to us, when we come home

from our chores at the immaculate glass hotel. We sip hot
coffee from thick white saucers while sitting on the porch.

We pray for the lost, when the wind rattles the windows
 or a big-bellied plane lifts the rows of silent people

into the night sky. We rise with the sun from our warm,
soft beds. *Let's eat corn*, our pretty boy sings.

BOARDWALK IN WINTER

The arcade paranoiac hoists a trophy of pulled-out
    roots above his feverish head.
The shaved monkey braves hunger and the wind

    for the gloved hand's stroke.
The child performer in his starched white shirt
    hacks at the strings of a frozen mandolin.

Bald Athena, shivering psychic, has a tooth that needs
    pulling and hammer toes in pink slippers.
She stows her rusty crown and files her nails grown wild.

the dark tree, the cold sea

although I know you can never be found
although I know that from the highest height
you cannot be seen you are not hiding
from me or are you is it how you look now
or maybe how I look now all these years gone by
places seen people met not knowing at any time
who I was or how others saw me or did not see me
and how are you wherever you are if I write you a letter
I'll get no answer if I cry out to you to come in my final
hour you will not come but I will still look for you

Selected Poems from
Hostage

NEMESIS

The old men with too much gamble in them, whose eyes

Are at peace only when all is lost, see the Queen's quiet face

On the deck of cards, the red cuff of her cloak, the raw tip

Of her tongue, the blood on her dress . . . What fled from them

In their frenzies comes tiptoeing back, choiring, to the marble

Concert hall where Nemesis, in velvet opera cape, is beginning

Her recitative: *it is your turn to go slowly now, with hands*

clasped behind your back, drowsy from the earth's sweet

abundance and her great deprivations, the rows of crooked trees,

the streets' bright monotony, to gather up the starving . . .

BACH FUGUE

Frees the horses from their mechanical bolts,

Keeps the fire from spreading to the sleepers' floor.

The miming dancers in the wings (*swell to great*)

Begin their sly whisperings, their tired arms

Around each other's waist. The old woman spoons yellow cake

Into her (*celestial tremulous*) mouth. Is capable of putting

Poor Gloucester's eyes, glistening, back. Catches the jumpers

With invisible nets from their sad, night bridges;

Finds all those who have been lost to you. The great

Chords, once struck, can never decay.

HORSEHEAD AT A PARISIAN FAIR

You are still in your face
Where the sun warms your mouth that once bit a mare's
In death-defying pursuit
In the memory of your standing, your fetlocks
Flecked with gold and white
At the flies that arrive full force to gnaw on you
You could almost toss your mane
Much as you would like to move, you look back at everything
In your path with glassy eyes, the mind of a quadriplegic
And of all that is captive
When you died, they placed you on your side
And bent your legs for running

KYRIE

The goal posts are off-kilter and the moon slides into my shoes.
I could disappear into the night like a hitcher,
Firebird of cinders,
Lost dogs, rising from their urine-soaked bedding
To await their human names.

In the dark cells, Beato Angelico's angels stream,
Spirals of pure solace, iodine weavings;
And the shining bodies draped in cloth,
Hands and feet missing, are
Feeling the dance in their mouths.

19 CHOPIN WALTZES

Snow falls from rafters of pink, swollen clouds;
moonlight drenches the peasants' fields.

The feathered flesh of a fish, the juice of a peach,
the silver rivers before we named them with color.

All the begetting: the weak limbs and soft bellies,
the faces elongated like the devil himself. The devil

himself! The ship that sails to dreams of Achilles,
the palace of the deaf, the murmuring in centuries' rooms,

the crying of turtle doves, the fleet-footed dancing.
On Earth as in heaven, beauty without reason.

BEAST OF BURDEN

piled so high the legs buckle
hit with a thin stick whistled at
shouted at kicked with their heels

end me
on this earth with these humans
under a boiling sun with rocks

remove the tower of wooden collar
studded with bells
from round my thick neck
so that removed
from all halters I may wander

let the dust blow me away
to long quiet roads
the clip clop of my feet
the only music I hear

or let me be gently lead like the old
or pull the wooden cart of babies
and nothing more

Lord of the Ass
lay me down
unencumbered in your green pastures
for which they incessantly pray

the air cooling and petting the bones of my ears
brushing my skull
the still waters washing out
my braying mouth

KAFKA'S SISTER

. . . but here is my Ottla, so alive inside her dressing gown,

her breasts like lady apples. See how she bends to pick up

Puss 'n Boots and bring him to her mouth, kissing him

on the rump! (That I were that cat!) How funny she finds me,

seated in my straight-backed chair, fastidious in overcoat,

gloves and bowler hat. "You look like you've seen a ghost,"

she is laughing. "So Franz!" Banished from my kingdom,

all icy winter and future's grief, now that she is here, her

dark hair falling down and around her face and the animal.

AWAY

The faint, hoarse breathing of a near-ghost sliding her arms

into a coat's listless sleeves. Just where does she think she is going in

that mothy thing, with a filthy stray shoved into the pocket, mumbling,

casting elephant shadows along the black walls of blind alleys,

crumbling buildings, a padlocked lumber yard, the dump,

and farther out, the red-lit hut with psychic inside, until

where, on the edge of the dark city, nothing more is.

SILENT MOVIE

Suddenly all the pedestrians and street vendors

are actors in the new silent movie: *The Horse that Stole*

Our Hearts and Galloped Off the Cliff, Its Iron Hooves

Pawing. Quickly, by the North Gate, for the city

is in flames and we will all perish! The horses are pulled

by ropes round their necks. The old grip tree trunks.

The newly arrived from dung-filled lands are grabbing up

cheap wool gloves, rubber boots, golden doorknobs

and going with hands clenched. Gap-toothed women

squeeze every cherry in the box with swift, nimble fingers.

THE LAST CIRCUS ON EARTH

At the last circus on Earth, papier-mâché parrots are strapped
To each child's wrist. A human elephant with a broken back, one man in front,
One in the back, makes a jaunty, grand entrance to the faint roar of the crowd.

Les Frères Mahoudeau, who have spent each entire morning mending
Their tattered tights, ballet slippers and fish net, for nothing but this matters,
Are making their tremulous way up the broken rope ladder.

The night watchman has cut loose the bear with a chained ring through its snout,
And the plumed, trick poodles, and run away with the woman who gets sawed
In half. The stuporous contortionist drowses inside the clown's yellow barrel.

INSOMNIA

Here comes the sweeper of the square

With his dry, straw broom, and even the scuttling rats

And the pigeons, with their insatiable bellies,

Their ravenous mouths, have a place to go.

Every gold and crimson Mary holds her son,

Nesting, with his old man's face, thin lips and sharp nipples

On a pale chest. Even the chained lie down in the dark;

Soldiers, sick of shoveling muck and trench, dream of resting

Beneath blankets of snow. The herder grips tight the squirming

Sheep and shears it down to its pink, quivering skin.

INTO GREAT SILENCE

Most humble, they answer to the ringing of the bell
and course down the stone halls to eat together: celery broth,
baguette, pears, hard cheese. Their brown robes sail like wings

behind them. After, the old monk, hunched, climbs
the narrow stairs with a basket balanced on the precipice
of his back to feed the strays, banging on the metal dish

and calling out to them like an owl. The cats come in all their hues
and patterns to the hoo-hooing and set to the brimming food
with loud licks. The cows, sheep, and flocked birds wait for

the humans who have lost their tongues to bring seed and straw
and no fear whatsoever. There are deep prints in the overnight snow
and from a distant valley comes the echo of a peacock's squall.

If you go into town, say the orders, you must neither eat nor drink
what is graciously offered but rest by the plain, wayside stream.
Cup your hands, brothers, and drink from the plain, wayside stream.

THE BLIND ARE SLEEPING

Their heads tilt gently on the pillows of the field.
Their hands, gesturing at the out-of-sight

with inexhaustible fingers, rest still as cats—
self-contained, melancholy—beside their prone masters.

The emptied body accommodates the most mottled flesh,
the most hapless limp. The blood that stops is rich

and tender. The aroma of wet grass and turf upturned
is the odor of young men, flavor of salt storm, of shout.

The sun still above is huge and boiling. The heads of the blind
warm like stones, their pale stares mesmerized, forever entering.

Their faces, unadorned, are devoid of human adoration.
Their mouths part as if they could almost sing.

Let me breathe you, says the choirmaster, who paints eyes
on their lids, and the blind who sleep—fly out.

MUSES

The Muses are giving a thousand poets, painters, dancers
The back of their hands, and having flown, seat themselves
On the hypnotically spinning stools of Hartley Farms
Where they are mouthing the giant menu with tremendous glee:
Raspberry swirl, chocolate marshmallow fudge, swiss mocha almond . . .
And motioning for Marina and Sophia in their green-and-white aprons
With fictive cows grazing, and leaning over the counter on alabaster white arms,
Whispering, "Girls, do not despair, ever, for we are here," so that the tired
Servers swipe their dark, perspired hair from their faces and wonder
Who is speaking, who is near and what in the world is forever.

THE CELLAR

Under the locked grille, the animals are crying.

You hear them while you wait and when the bus pulls up,

Finally, and you get on. That was years ago. The cellar

Is given over to new shopkeepers, one after the other,

Who fail and are replaced. Even the selfish brother,

The crazed neighbor, the criminal in his cell, face of blue

Tattoos, has never allowed a living thing to starve

As you have. Who knows this except for you and the laughing

African with his padlock teeth and flashing gold key.

HOSTAGE
for W. S. Merwin

God is in the dogs
The one who turns in circles, the one
With scabs, the one who wears the collar
Who stares and stares
And tries in spite of it to smell the dirt and grass
In the abandonment, torrential muteness
My knees loosened, my glassy eyes of crystal warmed
And it was given
Even should we sleep
Turn weep recite, screaming, "the city is conquered and the little king
Will have to go," insane and unreachable
We are still here

NOTRE DAME DE PARIS

What gusts of raw, mad emotion, of unbearable expectation, in this world-cutting-loose of the bells. A crucifix, fashioned of twigs, is being held up to all the draculas, who, convulsed, are going up in smoke to a shriek. Quaking birds are calling for assembly and their plaintive crying is being carried over the voice of the gun. Now the dead are stepping out of their wet shoes, and loosened from their withered chords, are calling to us from the deck of their boat: *Bon voyage, mes chers*! We are beside ourselves: *in ekstasis!*

LAZARUS, COME OUT

The sisters are wailing, quite beside themselves with something new.
The pale Christ, lanky as a long-distance runner, seems half-amazed
at what he has done. Sitting up, the awakened one sees the immobile

face of the woman he mounted like a maniac, his body erupting in fever,
in abscess, for want of her, and is indifferent. He can hear the murmurs,
the jeers and coarse laughter on the roads and in the homes, the crush

of a slapped face, the unhinged bells, the dangerous, sullen gaps.
Suddenly visible are the closed faces of the doomers and the open faces
of the doomed, although he is a dark room, his tongue black and stiff.

Fanatics who worship the sun sever their arms as offerings
to help it rise; it rises, and the disinterred one, for a time, continues,
dancing by himself like a horse with its screaming, high-tossing head.

APOLLO'S KISS

Devise Cassandra. Become her, in possession,
And the world becomes perfect. For even gods
Crave perfection. Desire her like a man
And like a man be refused in all your desire.
Surrender: beg a first and last kiss and pray
She will acquiesce, her virtue stirred.
Then, breathe into her mouth the powered
Prophecy and for all you are losing
—the deprivation she will give and give—
Release her half gifted, as you are, half mortal.

In the courtyard, animals are captured
By their hind legs, held up on haunches,
Throats slashed. She walks on burning
Stones. Swift, it is slaughtering season.

[EXIT, PURSUED BY A BEAR.

The callous henchman is the one devoured, the baby saved.
The wind picks up and sends the lazy dove-sails flying over waves

without a finger raised. Even the starved mongrel, abandoned
by your brother, pries open the ash can with its dirty snout

and finds a roasted chicken sitting right on top. Old-timers, every limb
aching to be straightened, march like pins. The torn angels are being fitted

for new gowns by the seamstress with cold lips. Turn, she mumbles. Turn,
the lovelies. The sun is granting her people a golden day, for no earthly reason.

CHERNOBYL

Crossing in the wrong direction, we are quickly

Sealed off, directionless, earth's blind villagers.

We follow the leader and the riverbank to its dried-out

Roots, while at the merest ruffle of wind, bird, leaf,

We hide ourselves behind the thick bodies of old trees

That have the tiny, sad eyes and the long, delicate lashes

Of chained elephants. We witness the quiet lives

Of fireflies, igniting themselves, their enviable wings;

The languorous butterfly climbing into the flower's face;

And begin to be muted by our arrival at the inconceivable

Door as when the radiated wolves crept into the hunters'

Huts to be comforted and were comforted.

HOST

There are two worlds I know of:
the vast illumined
and the place where I am.

I need the other
the way a virus
needs a host,
but the strange,
loving sisters
hold up their hands.

And my body—
uninhabited—
suffers and wonders:
Whose hands are these?
Whose hair?

GLENN GOULD, DEAD AT 50

It is darker where I am.
I cannot tell, holding my hand
over one eye, if it is female there.

At six,
I multiplied endlessly
and began to feel close
to sacrifice.

The music took root
inside, like torture,
all tension, ritard, release.

It is in every part
of my body now, and there is not
room left for me.

I have burned
all my capes, got rid of my papers.

THE SCARLATTI SUN

The mute seamstress on her knees
sticks a pin in the hem
and weeps for the cloth;

the dead stop their dying,
their heads warming like stones
in the Scarlatti sun,

while the grave postman,
his worn leather bag strapped to his back,
feels his mind go, windswept.

An old woman at her window,
her old cat on the sill, sips thick coffee
from a saucer, and in the shuttered convent,

the novitiate, taken up,
rushes across the just-washed floor,
daring the ground to break a bone.

More Praise for Emily Fragos

"Emily Fragos is a thin-skinned, tough-minded poet of this world. Her sensual sensibility is unrestrained by conventional perceptual grids. Her poems take us by surprise . . . Fragos's trust in language is fruitful, justified. No word she writes is an advertisement for herself. The out-going empathy which moves her now and then even allows her moments in which persons, acts, things, and self are poised as if reconciled. We are enlarged by her resonant verbal imagination."

—*MARIE PONSOT*